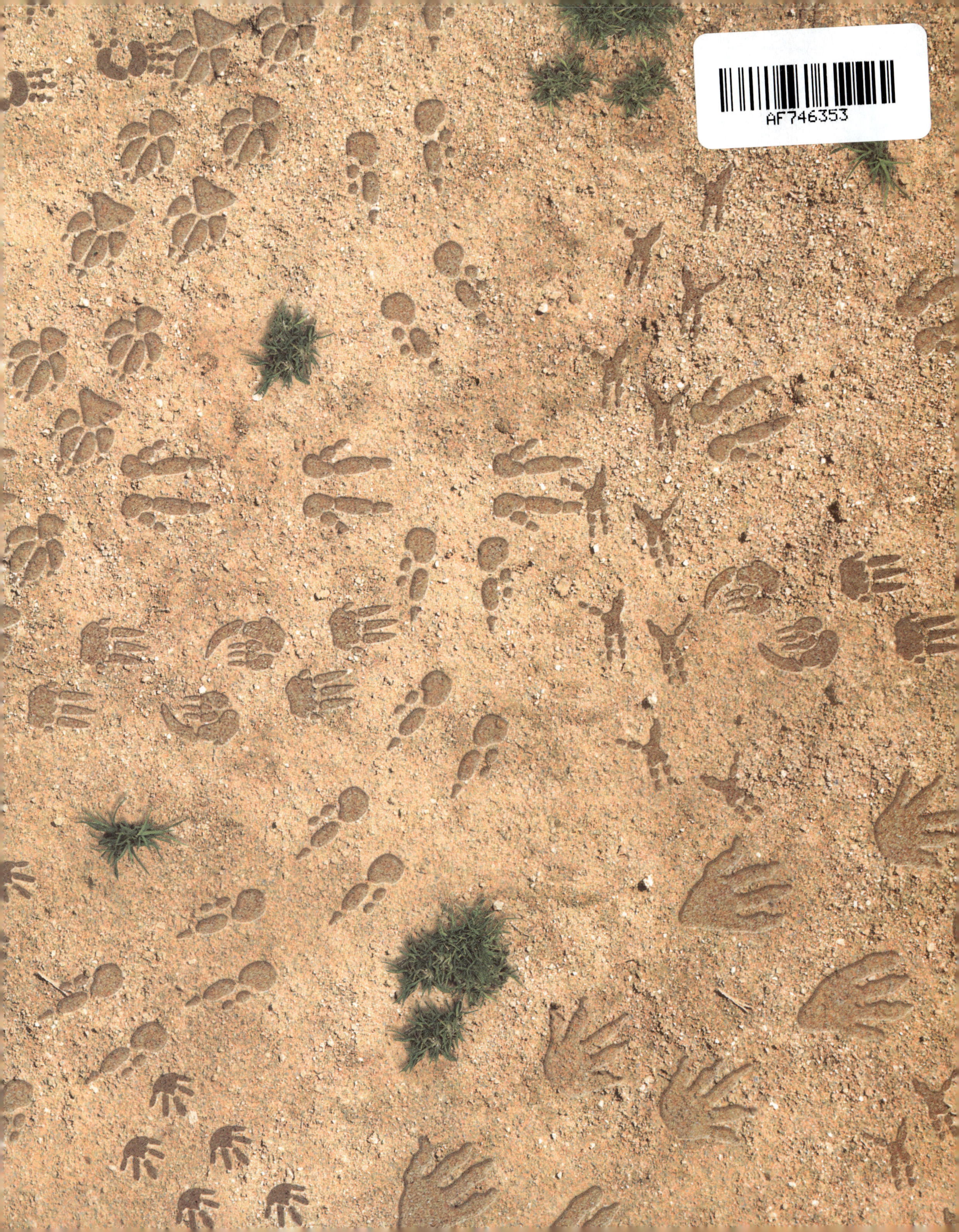

JOHN LESLEY

AUSTRALIA'S REMARKABLE WILDLIFE

BLUE-RINGED OCTOPUS

REDBACK publishing

First Published 2023 by
Redback Publishing
PO Box 357 Frenchs Forest NSW 2086
Australia

www.redbackpublishing.com
orders@redbackpublishing.com

978-1-925860-99-3_

ISBN 978-1-925860-99-3 HBK

Author: John Lesley
Editor: Caroline Thomas
Design: Redback Publishing

NATIONAL LIBRARY OF AUSTRALIA
A catalogue record for this book is available from the National Library of Australia

Original illustrations © Redback Publishing 2023
Originated by Redback Publishing

Printed and bound in Malaysia.

Acknowledgements
Abbreviations: l—left, r—right, b—bottom, t—top, c—centre, m—middle
p10 lb - Mark Anthony Sefuentes, p12-13 - Cromo Digital, p12c - Rickard Zerpe, CC BY 2.0 <https://creativecommons.org/licenses/by/2.0>, via Wikimedia Commons, p14l - NegKafou_Photography, p30bl - Pecold.
We would like to thank the following for permission to reproduce photographs: (Images © shutterstock), p10bl Mark Anthony Sefuentes, p12cm Cromo Digital, p12cl Rickard Zerpe, via Wikimedia Commons, p14tl NegKafou_Photography, p30bl Pecold.

Every effort has been made to contact copyright holders of any material reproduced in this book. Any omissions will be rectified in subsequent printings if notice is given to the publisher.

CONTENTS

The blue-ringed octopus has two types of venom in two separate venom glands. One is used when hunting food.

The other type of venom is extremely toxic and only used for defence.

When it first hatches, the blue-ringed octopus is the size of a pea.

BLUE-RINGED OCTOPUS BASIC FACTS

SCIENTIFIC NAME

There are four different types of blue-ringed octopus that have so far been named. Three of them are found in the waters that surround Australia.

All of them are in the group called *Hapalochlaena*:

- Southern blue-ringed octopus
- Blue-lined octopus
- Greater blue-ringed octopus

Squid

DID YOU KNOW?

Octopuses are related to squids (which are what we eat when we are having calamari for dinner).

TYPE OF ANIMAL

The blue-ringed octopus is a mollusc. Oysters and snails are also molluscs, but the octopus is different from them because it has lost its outer shell. Scientists call octopuses cephalopods (which means an animal whose head and foot are combined). All cephalopods are invertebrates, since they do not have a backbone.

BLUE-RINGED OCTOPUS BODY

COLOUR

The sandy or brown colour of the body quickly changes if this octopus feels threatened. Very bright blue rings then instantly appear all over its body. These are a warning to stay clear, both to people and to any other predator in the ocean. The display of these rings means that the octopus is about to release its poison into anything that touches it.

BRAIN

The octopus brain is shaped like a doughnut, and their gut passes through the hole in the doughnut. Octopuses are very intelligent and can learn behaviours that seem amazing for a creature related to snails.

EYES

Octopuses have the most advanced eyes found in any invertebrate animal.

SIZE

The body of the blue-ringed octopus is about the size of a ping pong ball, with eight legs that grow to around six centimetres long. The legs all grow around the mouth, which has a tiny, sharp beak. Despite this octopus's small size, don't be fooled into thinking it is so cute and tiny that you want to touch it!

ARMS

The eight arms can change shape, from being short to long, depending on how the octopus needs to move.

BLOOD

Blue-ringed octopus blood is blue because the chemicals in it are different from those we have in our red blood.

ARE THEY REALLY DANGEROUS?

VENOM

Venom is another name for the poison some animals produce. The blue-ringed octopus uses its venom for two purposes. The venom kills prey, such as crabs and fish, and it can also be a weapon to use against any creature that threatens the octopus by getting too near it.

The venom has killed people who were bitten. It causes a person to feel very sick, and may make them stop breathing. The venom is similar to that of the highly poisonous puffer-fish.

The tiny beak that forms the mouth of the blue-ringed octopus makes its bite not very painful to humans. Because of this, a person who is bitten may not realise it until they start to feel sick. As the octopus bites, it releases the venom into the wound from tiny sacs around its mouth.

HOW FAST ARE THEY?

A blue-ringed octopus can move around in two main ways. It walks around over rocks and coral in the ocean, using the suckers on its eight arms.

It can also push its body through the water by forcing water out of a funnel that is near its head. This quick movement is useful for escaping predators.

BLUE-RINGED OCTOPUS HABITAT

Found throughout the warm parts of the Pacific Ocean, the blue-ringed octopus lives in rocks pools and on shallow rocky areas. It is a marine creature, which means it lives in seawater and cannot survive in lakes or rivers.

It likes to hide in a burrow amongst rocks, where its normally sandy colour provides it with good camouflage. Sometimes, instead of finding a place to make a burrow amongst rocks, the blue-ringed octopus will hide in discarded shells or even cans and other human rubbish. It has an amazing ability to squeeze its whole body into a narrow space, which keeps it safe from predators.

NOT A GOOD PET!

It is not a good idea to keep a blue-ringed octopus in a fish tank at home. It will be very good at escaping and will bite if you find it and try to put it back in the water. Cleaning the tank is almost impossible as the octopus may bite if you put your hand into the tank.

BLUE-RINGED OCTOPUS LIFE CYCLE

The female makes a home which is like a small burrow amongst rocks. She hides from predators there, and waits at the entrance until prey comes past. She also looks after her eggs there.

EGGS

The female guards her eggs until they hatch, which may take some months. During this time, the female does not eat, and becomes weaker and weaker. Once the eggs are hatched, the female dies. She only lays eggs once in her lifetime.

BABY OCTOPUSES

The baby octopuses look after themselves, swimming around and catching tiny shrimp, or eating pieces of crab left over from another animal's meal. During this time they are very likely to be eaten by other creatures, such as fish and crabs. Only a few of the babies survive long enough to become adults that can breed and produce the next generation of babies.

After hatching, they first float around in the water, and later sink to the seabed. They find a safe place to protect themselves from predators, and come out to hunt for food or to find a mate when they are older.

LIFE SPAN

Blue-ringed octopuses may live for between half a year to about two years.

MATING

After the male and female mate, the female then produces about 100 eggs that are each the size of a pea. The male dies after it has mated with the female.

FOOD CHAIN

WHAT DOES A BLUE-RINGED OCTOPUS EAT?

It eats small fish, crabs and crustaceans, such as shrimp and prawns. To catch its food, it may hide and then pounce on a crab, or it may swim quickly to chase a shrimp.

The blue-ringed octopus inserts poison into its prey by biting it with a hard beak that forms its mouth.

The poison it inserts makes the prey stop moving so the octopus can eat it easily.

The shells and other pieces left over from the meals are usually scattered around the entrance to the burrow, giving a blue-ringed octopus its own little garbage dump.

Blue-ringed octopuses eat crustaceans like shrimp

Blue-ringed octopuses hunt small fish

WHAT EATS A BLUE-RINGED OCTOPUS?

Many animals in the sea know not to eat something with flashing blue rings on it, and they seem to have learned that this one is poisonous. Despite this, there are some animals that are not affected and will eat blue-ringed octopuses. These include eels, sharks and seabirds.

Even baby blue-ringed octopuses have venom, but it is a tiny amount. They are eaten by predators that play a role in controlling the numbers of blue-ringed octopuses in the ocean.

HOW DO THEY COMMUNICATE?

BLUE RINGS

The blue rings on the surface of this octopus only appear when it is threatened. There are tiny muscles in its skin that can make the blue rings appear or disappear, so they seem to be flashing on and off. This is a warning sign to any predator to stay back or get bitten.

INK

Larger octopuses have a big ink sac. They can shoot this black ink out of a funnel to confuse a predator. Blue-ringed octopuses have tiny ink sacks that are not of much use in producing enough black ink to shield their owners from danger. Instead, they use their potent poison to protect themselves.

TOUCH

Octopus arms are very sensitive, and are used to touch the surroundings and other octopuses.

WHERE TO SEE A BLUE-RINGED OCTOPUS

Around the Australian coast in rock pools or under water in shallow seas

On display in public aquariums

Some people may keep Blue-ringed octopuses in home aquariums, but the experts do not recommend doing this.

Q

They are so little. Surely they can't be so dangerous?

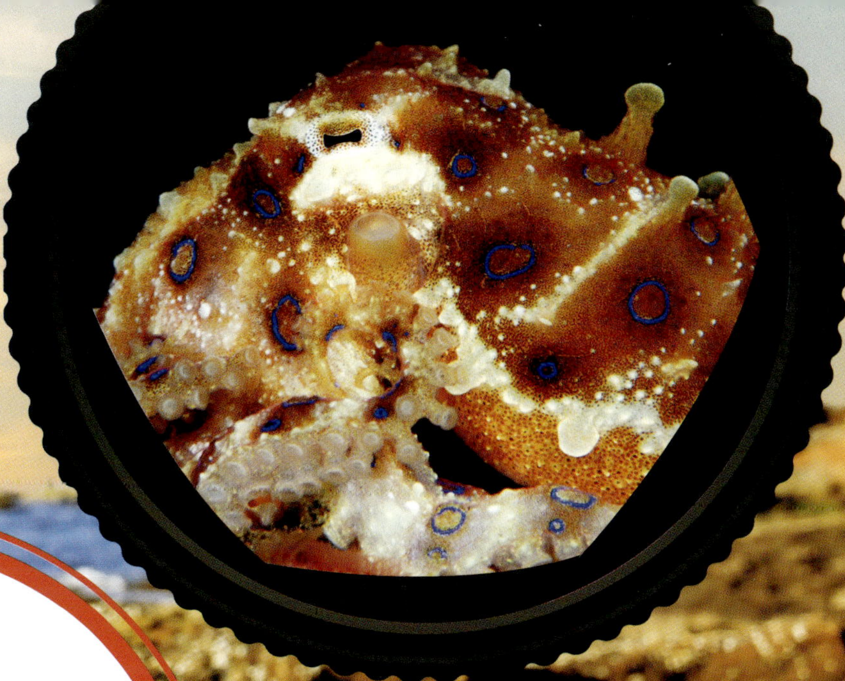

A

WRONG!
Blue-ringed octopuses are very, very dangerous. Size is not always a good way to tell whether you should beware of an animal or not.

BLUE-RINGED OCTOPUSES AND THE ENVIRONMENT

CLIMATE CHANGE

Warming seas will affect every living thing in them. A change in overall temperature affects sea life in two ways. The animal itself may get sick, but its food source may also be affected, so the animal starves.

RUBBISH IN THE OCEAN

Although blue-ringed octopuses live in burrows they find in rocks on the sea floor, or amongst corals, there is so much rubbish in the ocean and in rock pools, that they also make use of this when looking for places to hide.

Bottles and cans in the water around the shoreline may be homes to little blue-ringed octopuses, so take care if you are taking part in a clean-up campaign.

THE FUTURE OF BLUE-RINGED OCTOPUSES

The IUCN Red List of Threatened Species is an international list of the world's threatened animals, fungi and plants. In 2021, they had not listed any species of blue-ringed octopus as being endangered.

This does not mean that they are safe. Researching such a tiny creature is difficult, and whether it is endangered or not is still not known for certain.

Blue-ringed octopus hiding in a plastic bottle

SORTING ANIMALS INTO GROUPS

Biologists divide all living things around the world into groups. They call this process classification.

VERTEBRATES are what we call the group of animals with a backbone.

INVERTEBRATES

are what we call the group of animals without a backbone.

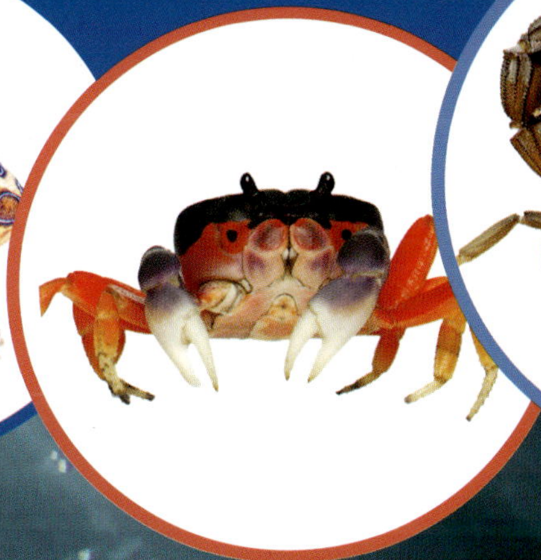

BLUE-RINGED OCTOPUSES ARE INVERTEBRATES

Some invertebrates, like crabs and insects, have hard, outer shells that give their bodies shape and strength. Octopuses do not have any bones inside their bodies and they have no hard, outer shell. They move and make their arms change shape by pumping fluid around inside themselves.

OCTOPUS ANIMAL RELATIVES

All of these creatures are in the same group of animals as the octopus: **MOLLUSCA**

Sea snail

Clam

Squid

Oyster

Slug

PEOPLE AND BLUE-RINGED OCTOPUSES

Although the venom of the blue-ringed octopus is so strong that it can kill people, many of those who were bitten did not even realise it. This is because the beak of the octopus is tiny. The venom can cause a person to become very sick and to stop breathing. There is no antitoxin at present.

This bad publicity has led some people to harm any blue-ringed octopus they find. This is not a sensible way to behave, as these tiny but dangerous creatures will not harm anyone as long as they are left alone.

Children playing around rock pools should keep well away from any little octopus they find, just in case it is a blue-ringed octopus. The blue rings will not appear until it becomes very angry at being disturbed.

Since it is so poisonous, the blue-ringed octopus is not taken by humans for food. The main threat to its future is from physical destruction of its habitat for building or reclaiming the ocean shores for human use. Climate change will also affect the habitat and the availability of its sources of food.

A few blue-ringed octopuses are taken from the wild for humans to display in aquariums.

HAVE I BEEN BITTEN?

People who have been bitten by a blue-ringed octopus report these reactions:

- Numbness at the site of the bite
- Being unable to talk or move
- Feeling dizzy and sick
- Having trouble breathing

A person who has been bitten needs medical attention quickly!

OCTOPUS IN MYTHS AND LEGEND

Throughout human history, the octopus has both terrified and fascinated people. Only a few hundred years ago, people believed that gigantic octopuses would attack sailing ships, killing everyone on board. Visions of long, octopus arms, covered in suckers, filled the nightmares of both sailors and passengers.

These stories probably grew out of the mythical Kraken, a giant octopus or squid in legends from Norway and Greenland.

In ancient Roman culture, about 2,000 years ago, octopuses were caught for food, as they are today. Pictures of them have been found painted onto the walls of rooms in buildings. They were also sometimes chosen as the subject for a mosaic decoration made out of tiles on the floor.

GLOSSARY

antitoxin treatment that overcomes the effects of a poison

camouflage body shapes or colours that help hide an animal

campaign organised actions to achieve a goal

cephalopod animal with a head and foot combined

classification process of sorting things into groups

gut part of body where food is processed

invertebrate animal without a backbone

marine referring to the sea or ocean

mating when a male and female come together to produce offspring

mollusc unsegmented invertebrate with a soft body and sometimes a shell

mosaic pattern made out of little tiles

numbness not being able to feel anything

potent powerful

predator animal that eats or attacks another animal

sac small pouch or container inside an animal's body

venom poison produced by an animal

INDEX